THE LITTLE RED BOOK

HOW TO DEFEAT GAMBLING & ADDICTION IN 7 DAYS OR LESS

Copyright

The Little Red Book

Santos Rolon Jr

Santosrolon@soldiersofselfmastery.com

Dedicated to...

Contents

INTRODUCTION

Want to become the best version of you? Read This Book Often! You can fulfill your life's mission. If I can, you can!

Follow your heart, my friend? Work on making it purer. I will be a co-partner with you in all of this. One thing before we continue with this Little Red Book journey. Right off the bat, I'm going to ask you to say this to yourself out loud right now: "I believe that something great will come to me (you name it) using what breakthrough Coach Santos has shared with me from this book." Say it yet? Great Job! Let's go forward.

It all started with one question. How can I find God's will for my life? After my honorable discharge from the US Navy in 1993, something was missing, without a sense of fulfillment. Desperately looking for the answer, I began a journey to find my purpose.

I stirred up desire mixed with hope. Through overcoming a dark, painful addiction to problem gambling for more than 32 years, little did I know I would discover other harmful habits that would be defeated also. It was like waking up and ending a long episode of horrible nightmares. I began to understand what would be my life's mission.

To Jesus Christ, in all humility, I give all the praise! Special thanks to my wife, Sherry, my children, who helped me build patience, Ines, the young lady, mom, pop Santos Sr, Cephas Tope, my business partner, and Diane, who shared some helpful writing tips with me on this revised project.

"This is the latest improved version" of The Little RED Book. A special, big thanks to all of you who purchase the book. You are all helping my mission go forward, to inspire thousands into an awareness of their most enormous potential. Thank you for permitting yourself to take the necessary action to bring to an end problem gambling and/or addictions in your life; you are courageous!

Even though this book may read like it's just for problem gambling, it's not! We all have negative habits that hold us hostage, from overeating, harmful anger, and anything in between. Within this book is your universal application, a solution to master your mind and train your brain to live a clean life and sustain success in the long run.

I encourage you to start keeping a journal, keeping notes, or, as I like to call it, "journaling." An essential step toward personal progress. You're building a positive habit that will help you develop the best version of yourself and bring about a total transformation in your life.

Most successful people have a way of keeping notes or journaling. Another thought to consider is that when you write a thought about a particular idea ringing in your head, it will help you come back to that frame of mind so you can further develop that idea later.

If you come across an exercise that does not resonate with you, go to the next section, you can go back to the difficult one later on. Friend, your mind is creative, and through persistence, it will reveal your solution.

Have you ever considered how you became who you are today? How have you made it through difficult life experiences? How did you keep thriving when others have lost it and have faded away in the face of the challenges you're facing right now? Have you ever given this serious thought? I never considered it necessary to think about these things until I experienced a personal transformation. I never knew what it meant to sit down and think. It was a new awareness as I began to construct a new foundation for personal growth and success in life.

You do want to move away from negative habits and addictions to achieve a positive transformation, right? Into a better understanding of yourself, which is your foundation for growth. What's negative in your life, why? Why do you do the things you do? Here is my philosophy on this subject.

The words addiction and habit are almost interchangeable; both terms can describe a positive or harmful activity.

Lifestyle is a byproduct of habits. Habits or addictions result from your repetitive actions.

These repetitive actions are the results of certain family traditions and experiences that we are exposed to early on during our first years of coming into this world.

As we grow, and once we can think on our own, we either add or remove certain beliefs as we begin to make personal choices in life.

We must get into a habit of challenging ourselves, our experiences, and our values at a foundational level before becoming a part of our daily living or influencing us.

Understanding this is very important today, now more than ever, as parents, especially if you are growing a family.

As you study the contents in this short book, you should experience a new awareness in your mind, a bit of a battle of thought. If you run from this, you will miss out on your true blessing, which is disguised within this experience. To experience self-improvement, there has to be a transformation within your mind.

A scribe wrote: “Be ye transformed by the renewing of your mind.”

Simply put, you have to be willing to let go of negative beliefs and allow positive new ones to flow in. In due time, you will win more mind battles with ease by focusing on building positive habits. It’s like opening a door and stepping into a new journey that will have mountain top bliss and down in the valley lows. And you will be tested. What you learn on the mountain top will be tested in the valley.

Remember that first job? That first date? That first new experience you became confident about after some practice? Like leaving home to be on your own? At the beginning of every great journey, there is going to be some kind of challenge.

That’s why what I share with you will go against most of your current beliefs, and that’s exactly what’s intended here. Changing your mental record, developing a winners mindset. The result? The best ‘you’ is being created through this process!

This is not a feel-good book. Though some parts of it are fun, my primary intention here is to give you reasonable, provoking thoughts and exercises, so you experience a total transformation and breakthrough throughout your journey as you apply what stands out to you from this book. You know, just like gold has to be purified through fire, I want you to experience personal change so you can go forth like pure gold.

It's exciting when you are more ALIVE! And more in control. More alive means more courage, more vision, and more awareness resulting in victorious daily living.

I recommend that you spend a day on each Chapter and do all of the exercises. If you do that, in 7 days, you'll have the tools and abilities you need to defeat gambling and any other horrible addiction. Let's get the journey started.

CHAPTER ONE: An Honest Confession: A Bit Of My Story And How I Achieved A Breakthrough From Gambling

---

During my childhood years, I experienced a lot of domestic violence; there were a few days when things appeared to be calm. Most of my early development was full of fear, violent threats of death or suicide, and physical and verbal abuse, especially against mom.

One event almost took mom's life. All this happened because my father was a distant, mysterious person. So growing up, I lived with constant fear, which subconsciously sabotaged my confidence and progress of success. Escapes became a normal routine, which resulted in negative experiences, via pills, pot, alcohol, if other different drugs were available those too would be tried. Promiscuity was easy to develop in those days too.

What you focus on is what you will bring into your life. Research shows that our beliefs or group paradigms develop into habits very early on. Your lifestyle is like a hypnotic state or like a trance. I agree with this reasoning. It is possible for us unknowingly or knowingly to put ourselves in a state or situation that causes us to move in a specific direction whether good or bad. Does it make sense to understand this, especially today?

It's very frightening, not knowing the kind of deposits and belief systems that can enter your mind from conception and as your subconscious is being trained from an almost magical influence from the behaviors of close family and friends until about 7 or 8 years of age. It could be a higher age since there is no direct information that proves 100% that it's only a 7 or 8 year period of intake. The key thing I want you to understand here is that early-stage deposits create the deepest, strongest habits in your life. Our values are formed very early on. And sometimes, they don't show up until later on in our life. It's amazing what we find that holds us back and sometimes we didn't even know it was inside of our head.

Truth be told, we can't easily erase habits and beliefs that are dropped from our family members or that come into our life as a result of our environment or group thinking. When you're a child, you don't have any choice in the matter of a lot of the stuff that's going into your head. It's really cool how we begin to identify these limiting beliefs (A light turns on!) and we can challenge them to become our best!

Can you relate to what I am sharing here? About why you are where you are? And why do you behave in some way that's different from someone else? I am not an expert in behavioral science; I explain these things as I have experienced them in my life and as I see them in others.

Developing a better understanding of your existence and why you do the things you do will help you in more ways than you can ever imagine.

There are countless numbers of people living today that also have a similar story, just like mine or even worse! By the grace of God, I am one of those individuals that broke through and freed himself to begin this new journey that has led me to a much happier life.

One reason I enjoy educating others via a book, video, or through personal self-empowerment coaching is because of my mother's influence as a teacher and the transformation I've experienced.

Mom made deep-seated deposits in me while we lived during those dark years. I see them now as I look back from time to time. Mom is a miracle woman! Dad is also somewhat of a miracle as well. Both are still alive. Mom, at 75, is a retired educator living in Willimantic, Connecticut. Love you, mom! Dad is 73 and disabled and lives in Stockton, California, in a care facility. I get to visit him every day and make sure he is "Tranquilo" (At peace). Love you, dad! Mom and I have deep conversations these days about our journeys.

Even though I have had a rough childhood, and despite how difficult my dad was, Mom's words and encouragement helped me face my fears and helped me make positive decisions that led to the breakthrough I'm enjoying today.

You and I are privileged to have a few key people in our lives who are dreamers and achievers. It could be a mother or a father or a good friend or an extended family member. Let's learn and appreciate them, and spend time with them. Some folks don't have the privilege to be around great dreamers, but we do have access to their book or video. Influencers could be a video, a conversation, a friend, a journal, a life hack. Even a thought you write down. Once again I must say that none of this would be possible for me but for the grace of the Almighty, which goes for all of us.

Your Past Should Not Dictate Who You Are Today

Miles Davis Quote: "When you hit a wrong note, it's the next note that makes it good or bad."

Our apartment building consisted of six units on top of a hill not too far from an eerie, abandoned, red brick warehouse with many broken windows.

I had the rude pleasure of throwing rocks at the unbroken windows for fun. I know today it was not proper! Forgive me for breaking windows; it's well behind me now.

One evening while the family was cooling off in front of our apartment building as the sun was going down. I said the wrong thing to a family member that was visiting; my dad's sister.

Dad thought I deserved to be punished, which today is called abuse. I guess I did something deserving of being whipped with a tree branch that was snapped off a tree in the front yard. I can still visualize myself hopping in a circular motion as dad held me by one hand and lashed the back of my legs with that whip. I remember crying on my bed in my mother's arms, as my legs were feeling the welts.

These types of experiences went on and on for many years during my early childhood. We move on but emotional experiences are not easily forgotten. They lie and wait to do their work. People end up carrying the burden and bitterness for years, if not until death. No wonder so many people are bitter, scarred, and unforgiving today. In fact, a lot of people around you do not stop to think about what they are presently doing.

You might be saying, but Santos, you have no idea what I have gone through during my childhood. Yes, I agree. I resonate with that. I know experiences in life differ for everyone, but can I be frank with you for a moment? It doesn't have to define who you are or who you will become.

Even though you might find yourself living every single day of your adult life feeling inadequate, empty, attracted to wrong things, fearful, or made to feel dumb by others, including family members, as if you don't have what it takes to make things happen, this doesn't have to decide who you will become in life.

Simone Weil Quote: "Pain and suffering are a kind of currency passed from hand to hand until they reach someone who receives them but does not pass them on."

Nelson Mandela was convicted during the apartheid era in South Africa, an act that landed him 27 years in prison. After his release in 1990, he didn't seek revenge against his jailers; instead, he invited one of them, a white man named Christo Brand, to his 1994 presidential inauguration. In fact, Brand was also invited to Mandela's 20th-anniversary celebration of his release from prison. Another of Mandela's jailers, James Gregory, also spoke and wrote about his friendship with the political prisoner.

The key lesson here? When Mandela was the president, he had the power for revenge and could jail the jailers. He could have set a trap or manipulated them and sent them to prison as they did to him. Honestly, with

Mandela being the president, an act of successful revenge would be guaranteed.

But he did just the opposite. You and I can imagine what was going on in his mind. Instead of taking revenge, he decided not to let his past define his present. He chose to forgive and love wholeheartedly.

Later on, Gregory and Brand both spoke about their deep respect for Mandela -- Brand, specifically, has spoken about his transformation from a pro-apartheid young man into a man against racial segregation and oppression. Mandela's influence, according to Brand, was unbelievable and life-changing. For many around the world, Mandela's act has become a powerful lesson in forgiveness.

Whatever you're going through right now, you can choose to release the pain, forgive, and to let go. You are the one who has the right to decide who you'll become, not your past or the pain. To prevent more suicides from happening is also one of the primary reasons I wrote this book, so please remember this. You should think of how you will turn things around because you can. And right here is hope for a brighter day and a greater you.

My Breakthrough From Problem Gambling

After losing well over $500,000 to gambling, and only GOD truly knows how many hours I have given away, I found self-realization, which we will discuss in the next chapter, and is one of the key steps in my self-recovery journey. I began making changes. I was no longer satisfied with the life I was living, and I desired to leave a positive legacy for future generations. I began by asking myself these questions:

What is my God-given purpose?

How am I going to get this done?

What are my gifts and abilities?

Why am I alive today?

What do I want people to say about me when I am gone?

After asking myself those questions, solutions began unfolding before me. I started gaining ideas about what I could do to begin turning my life around. It was like coming out of a dark closet that I had been in for many years. A bubble I lived in. I experimented with many new different rituals (Life-hacks) until I realized changes. I defeated a secretive, very harmful addiction called problem gambling. Once you get your first life breakthrough, it will begin a fantastic journey of self-discovery and self-awareness into other personal breakthroughs almost automatically.

If you could play a game of trade with yourself, what would you give up? Imagine trading your negative addiction-habits for positive habits today, right now, where would you begin?

Write down the thoughts that come to your mind. These will become your goals. Now, what is the smallest step you can take today to start achieving those goals? The very first little step? Friend, it's time to make a brief foray into an actual reality.

CHAPTER TWO: The Power Of Self-Realization

I read the story of a man who had been down on his luck and was desperate to make a little money. After so many closed doors and failed attempts, the idea of going to the city zoo clicked; hoping to get a job feeding the animals. The manager at the zoo had no vacancies but seeing how big the man was, he offered him another possible option.

He said, "our gorilla died the other day and he was one of our popular exhibits. If we got you a special gorilla suit, would you put it on and imitate him for a few days, until the new gorilla arrives? We'll pay you well for it!"

"Well, when you need a job, you need a job," said the man in need. He was so desperate for work, he was ready to do anything as long as he could make ends meet and provide for his family. So he agreed to take the position.

Let's give our story a pause for a moment. Do you have any idea of the decisions people have to make once they find themselves in a tight spot, once they are desperate?

Of course, you know what I'm talking about, you've been there yourself, that point you lost your job and had to sit at home for what...
Weeks?
Months?
Or even years?

At that point, you had to make a desperate decision just like the man in the story. Your luck was down, you applied for many other jobs but had the door slammed at you so many times that you can't even begin to count. You have a family to take care of, or maybe you weren't even married yet, but you had to measure up to your peers. You tried everything there was to try from your perspective and then... gambling entered your life.

It wasn't too harmful the first time, as it was just a few bucks you put in and lost. The push came to get back your money and gradually from a few dollars you went on gambling what little savings you had, all of it. Now it's painful, but you can't let go, you want to get it all back and all you needed was your very good friend- LUCK!

Luck probably did show up and you won. But rather than quitting you thought, "this isn't so bad," so you went on and on, growing in debt, losing relationships, and losing yourself through the process.

You need a solution, to get you out of this sinking state you have found yourself in. You need a miracle! And you need it fast.

You're back to where you were at the beginning -- in desperation, but unlike before when you had to make a decision that cost you a lot, this time will be a whole lot different.

This book you're holding will help you, or rather put you on the right path to realize how much you can be, to become the best version of yourself by breaking old harmful habits, and building new helpful ones.

Back to our story, he did agree to take the position of the gorilla and in a matter of a few hours, he got into the suit and started playing his part, beating his chest and shaking the bars. He started getting attention from huge crowds gathering outside the bars. "Maybe this won't be a bad idea after all," he told himself.

The pay was pretty good and he had all the bananas he could eat, and when he thought about it, there were worse jobs than this out there.

But one day, just in the middle of his gorilla act, he was swinging on a trapeze and lost his grip. He landed in the middle of the lion's den. Looking up at this intruder in his territory, the lion roared. The crowds were mesmerized to be caught in this jungle scene, a big bad gorilla versus a ferocious lion.

What would the gorilla do? He realized that if he cried out for help, it would reveal his true identity, so he slowly walked backward away from the lion, hoping to climb the fence back into his cage. The hungry-looking lion started stalking him step by step, and finally, in desperation, the gorilla cried out, "Help!" Immediately the lion answered in an annoyed whisper, "shut up stupid! You'll get us both fired."

I hope that cracked you up a bit, 'cuz' you need it. Lighten up your mood, you're holding your solution in your hands, and everything will be just fine.

You've landed in the den of gambling addiction and you feel it stalking you, about to eat you up, but just like the story, it isn't real, it's all in your head. And that's where you want to start shifting your focus from what's not authentic to what is - your self-realization!

SELF-REALIZATION - YOUR KEY TO QUITTING THE GAMBLING ADDICTION.

The key to quitting gambling or any addiction is first to acknowledge it as a problem, or become aware that one is addicted and start working toward making changes. I could say that because you're reading this book right now means you have come to that realization and congratulations on taking this big step. A quantum leap into complete freedom from gambling or any other addiction you believe has you by your throat.

I want you to understand that this first step you have taken requires tremendous strength and courage! To own up to this, to come to the realization of addiction as a problem you are facing and doing your best to be rid of it, especially if you have lost a lot of money and have strained or broken relationships along the way are a testament to your courage.

Right now, you are frustrated, and in great despair. You feel like this is your cross, and you have to bear it alone, but here is good news for you.

What good news?

Yeah, you're probably very eager to hear good news, more importantly, news that will bring a solution.

The good news is that you are not alone, you might have lost everything, even your loved ones, but you're not alone in this situation. Many others have been in your shoes and have been able to break the habit and rebuild their lives. You can, too! And that's the reason I wrote this book to help you through this phase of rebuilding everything that has gone wrong and most importantly, enables you to break your addiction.

Believe me; it's an easy task, as long as you're ready to see it through to the end and to erase every doubt and fear. So, let's work together to help you recover all that you've lost in the past.

What Is Self-Realization?

Self-realization means knowing oneself, to realize the truth of one's existence, to reach your full potential.

I believe my self-realization journey started after hitting 'Rock Bottom' a few years ago. For many years before I hit rock bottom, I was flowing in and out of casinos and I was spending cash like I didn't have a future. I was cutting corners and living a lifestyle that was making me sick. I tried to hide from myself but that didn't work very well. I was getting beat up by these casinos and the slot machines week after week. Not only that, but I was also committing other different types of sins that seemed to be tied to this environment of living. Gambling is extremely destructive, just like any other bad habit that we don't break. I believed that I would never see the day out of gambling. That's how involved I was in that lie.

Hitting rock-bottom, was one of the best experiences that have happened to me. There is nothing more powerful than standing in the presence of a group of people and having full control over your thoughts and your speech and being fully aware of what's going on around you, even to the point where you're listening to your heartbeat and you are present. This is true self-realization, a work to be desired. I probably should mention here that pride will either destroy you or it will make you into a better person. It's something that we should constantly check within ourselves. Where is my pride taking me? Your pride might be blocking you from taking that very next step that you know you should be taking right now. Pride cometh before the fall; beware of pride.

Why am I alive today?

Think about this for a moment - when was the last time you asked yourself this question: why am I alive today? You can't afford to live your life just anyway you want; you know where that is going to lead you.

You should earnestly desire to experience life through defining your existence and to clearly see what the exact reason is that you were created and the answer to that is not to gamble away your life, or waste it, no! By no means! I often reflect on hours that I could have invested wisely. Nevertheless, I can still look back and learn, and share that experience with others.

There is a greater purpose as to why you are here on earth. When you have succeeded in finding this out and when you begin actualizing it, you will look at yourself and feel new fulfillment. You're a new person, you're actualizing your inner giant. Confidence, belief, inner peace, joy, and money come later!

THE MIND MOUTH POWER CONNECTION

M.M.P.C. In short, I created this slogan to signify tools of self-mastery for life-hacking rituals, which involve concentrated efforts on control and guidance of thought/Emotion and self-talk/Communication. I have been changing my behavior through M.M.P.C.

Years after asking myself the "who am I" question and what is God's will? I made a decision and trained myself with Self Mastery rituals, exercises, and life-hacks. I defeated a secretive, harmful addiction called Problem Gambling. I have convinced, retrained my mind, restored the control of my body through a new vision, and striving to fulfill my daily mission.

This for me, as I mentioned earlier, was like coming out of a dark closet that I had been in for many years. A bubble I had lived in. Once I got my first life breakthrough, it was the beginning of a fantastic journey of discovery and greater self-awareness.

Through the Grace of God, I am who I am today. I will continue to become a better version of myself, not a bitter version. I will continue to help others get from where I was with problem gambling to where I am now - a state of freedom from the grip of addiction. Believe with me!

ACHIEVING SELF-REALIZATION

I heard the story of a wealthy man who threw a party for his daughter because she was approaching marriageable age. He wanted to find a suitable spouse for his daughter, someone courageous, intelligent, and highly motivated. He, therefore, invited a lot of young eligible bachelors to the party.

After they had a wonderful time at the party, he took the suitors to the backyard where he had an Olympic-sized swimming pool filled with poisonous snakes and alligators. He announced, "whoever will dive into this pool and swim the length of it, can have his choice of one of these three things. One, he can have a million dollars, two, he can have ten thousand acres of my best lands or three, he can have the hand of my daughter in marriage, who upon my death will inherit everything I own."

No sooner had he finished talking, when a young man splashed into the pool and reappeared at the other end, in less than two seconds. The rich man was overwhelmed with the young man's enthusiasm and asked, "young man, I have never seen anyone so excited and motivated in my entire life, do you want the million dollars, 10,000 acres, or my daughter?"

The young man looked at him sheepishly and said: "Sir, I would like to know who pushed me into the pool!"

Lol! My friend, you are capable of more than you can imagine, whether you get a push or not, go for it! And experience your full potential coming into the limelight.

Maybe, I am giving you that push already because that is my mission right now. To shake you out of your present position, to encourage you to discover and uncover the unusual gifts and talents embedded within you.

Ask yourself this question, am I going to allow the harmful incidents and hopeless failures of my past to undermine my future?

No! Although, you've been through hard times, ones that I can't even imagine, right? But you have to put that behind you and take control of your life now!

FINDING YOUR PASSION- A KEY TO SELF-REALIZATION

"If you have a strong purpose in life, you don't have to be pushed. Your passion will drive you there."
— Roy T. Bennett.

If you ask most successful people, they will tell you the first step of their journey was finding their passion and following it through with all zeal and focus. Whether you think this has become a cliché or not, the thing is it's a real fact and no bluff at all.

It is your passion, your why, the dream that will keep you going when the road gets rough, and as you know, it does get rough.

So how do you find your passion? How do you discover that which brings you joy every day so you can live to your highest potential?

Answer these questions sincerely:

What are the five things I am naturally good at? (this can include the skills you've been recognized for in the past, as well as your accomplishments.)

What are five things that interest you every day? (the type of information that gets you engrossed daily, forgetting every other thing, whether through TV, blog articles, books, tapes, podcasts, magazines, etc.)

What kind of people do you spend your time with? (are they the kind to learn from positively, do they lift you or bring you down)

What five things bring you joy? (what gets you jumping off your bed in the morning, what makes you eager to start your day)

What do you have to offer others? (what need can you fulfill in others through your skills, what can you do for free, for most of us this is where your purpose lies)

I have something else for you, what are the five things you would do if you learned that you only had nine months to live?

Take some time to reflect on this and write your answers here.

1. I will____

2. I will____

3. I will____

4. I will____

5. I will____

Are you done with that yet? If you are great! If you skipped it, please go back and write your answers, or if you prefer you can reflect on it throughout your day. Think about your benefits from doing the exercises in this book. Own them, make them yours!

Phewww!!! That was a whole lot of work. Take a break from this book and give yourself a sweet treat, then come back refreshed!

Do not forget to reflect on these questions and the answers you've given, also think of how you can use them positively to create a better you.

CHAPTER THREE: Reinventing The Wheel

Hey! My friend, welcome back, what did you do while you were away? Did you go to the beach? Or did you hang out with some friends? Anyways, I hope you gave yourself a nice treat.

In the previous chapter, we succeeded in outlining your passion, that which brings you joy. That which interests you and gets you starting your day in excitement and that is going to lay the foundation of reinventing the wheel of your life.

To most people, the idiom, "reinventing the wheel" carries a negative meaning that includes wasting time and energy in creating that which already existed. But in this context, we are reinventing the wheel with incremental improvements.

What do I mean by this?

I mean that we are going to be recreating the life you had before your gambling addiction or any other addiction. But we are not just stopping there, we are also going to make it better than it was before.

Some of you don't agree with this, right?

Perhaps, your life before falling into problem gambling was a mess, and you certainly do not want to relive such an experience.

Very well then, you have the opportunity to choose and create a new life for yourself. Before we go further let's go on a history tour.

We will return to once upon a time when things were, maybe not perfect, but close to being real, a time before you lost your job or a time before you functioned without any addictions. All those times, you lived without the burden of debt, and those times you had a perfect dream of how your life would turn out. But unfortunately, you find yourself on the wrong side of life, frustrated, and wishing you had never decided to gamble in the first place. The question you now ask yourself is "How did I get here?" "How did I get into such a mess?"

Tell me, if you had an opportunity right now, to go back, to relive your life or to make new decisions and to choose better helpful habits, what would be your decision?

Well, I'm so sure you will jump at such an opportunity and believe me, anybody would!

We've all been victims of times when we had to make rash decisions, many of which cost us a lot later in life. So getting an opportunity to make things right again is gold and that's what I'm offering you right now. To recreate the experience you would prefer to live, to recover all the years you lost to your gambling addiction, including renewing the relationships that were strained along the way.

How can you rewire your brain to function healthy and to live a life free of any addictions?

All you need to do is acknowledge that gambling is an addiction that brings you no pleasure at all but rather only pain, and it has been proven that attaching pain to a particular habit automatically rewires your brain to avoid such habits.

Chances are you know your gambling addiction causes you pain, harm, and misery but each time you try to quit, you feel the compulsion to go back. You've succeeded in keeping anyone from knowing about your gambling problem because unlike other addictions such as smoking, drinking, and doing drugs, gambling has no physical effect, you just keep on pretending that everything is fine when it's not.

When you run out of money at times, you feel that compulsion to borrow again, probably from a friend or even your family members and you hope and pray they do not ask what you need it for and even when they do ask, you make up lies and stories just to get them to lend you the money to nourish your gambling urge.

As time goes on, you need to repay your debt because your friend or relation won't stop pestering you to get their money back. Now you lose their respect and trust. From wagering your money in the casino, you proceed to lose friends, family, your home, and so sadly some people even lose their life as a result of committing suicide.

I'm not trying to present a recap of how you've spent your life, neither am I trying to worsen your pain. I won't do that because I have been in your shoes and I feel what you feel right now.

But just for a moment, think of all you've had to face because of your gambling addiction, isn't that enough pain? Really think about it!

You cannot afford to go back and relive such a life, and that's why you probably picked up this book. You need a solution, you need a new life, and you have certainly done the right thing by picking up this book because it is the solution to your problems and answers to your questions.

MY EXPERIENCE WITH "REINVENTING THE WHEEL"

It was a new root problem in my childhood, which turned into a severe gambling lifestyle problem that lasted several decades.

After 40+ years of many bad decisions, (and a few, minor good ones) and several near-death experiences, along with a traumatized mindset, I could say (I have choices!) I began my first reinvention transformation by building my first few positive habits.

Through meditation on scripture, video therapy, positive self-talk, mirror talk, and other experimental life-hacks, I experienced my transformation. I am hoping you do too through these proven tips I am sharing with you here in this book. It has worked not just for me alone, but for many others who have watched my YouTube videos and joined my self-mastery class. And they all have experienced a great transformation in some form.

I am no longer a slave to the lie gambling tells, no longer drinking in the vomit of destructive lies, or feeding the coffers that were draining the life out of me, making excuses, and living a double life with horrible addictions.

It was a dark life, where I lost hundreds of thousands of dollars, wasted many hours of accountability by being away from my family and my responsibilities (I could have been so much more productive). I fabricated more lies, stole from Peter to pay Paul, which never fared well.

I have faced suicidal thoughts, depression, fear, hiding, loss of a good job, and being homeless with my family for at least 6 months; my second time being homeless. It paralyzed me in an induced hypnotic state of continuous defeat. The mental battle you go through is extreme, although there were good times and a few good decisions, the evil would always dominate because the evil wolf was getting the bigger portions of food, figuratively speaking. Whatever you focus on the most will definitely show up in your life.

I hope to get this book into the hands of as many people as possible. I know that there are people on the verge of committing suicide, and I continually fought against it. This book will bring you hope and may vigorously help you prevent that from happening. Your purchase helps me reach those people before it's too late.

I thank you from the bottom of my heart. You are a partner with me in this movement, which I call Soldiers of Self-Mastery. You may even consider purchasing an extra copy and giving it to someone you know and care about. This book makes a great gift.

Enjoy the manual and together let's get angry against the mental injustice of Self-destruction.

Are you living in a silent nightmare? If you are please remember this, you can overcome it, as I have.

To succeed, you must understand that all successful people fail at some point in their lives.

"Anchor your reason for doing what you need to be doing. It will keep you firm as you go through your storms from failure to success."

The Grace of God broke through allowing me to decide (please remember this, you have choices). I anchored my reason to reach this new man, to persist throughout, and with the practice of good life-hacks, I stopped gambling and developed confidence that almost made me feel sky-high.

Through experimenting and using the tools and ideas, I'm sharing with you in this book, it won't have to take you 32 years, a rock bottom experience, or some fatal accident that could lead to death for you to be on the better side. I've created a guideline for you and it has your name on it.

This is your manual, your life raft. You now have an excellent tool you can use daily.

The first tool I would like to share with you is what I call video therapy.

WHAT THE HECK IS VIDEO THERAPY? WILL IT HELP ME?

I want to bring the subject up right now before we proceed into other life-hacks because this has played a significant role in my transformation.

As I worked on my harmful addictions, I stopped watching TV, and I cut out a lot of the negative media news, along with a few people that weren't helping me.

I turned to Google and YouTube. I would spend countless hours when I wasn't working and most times throughout the day, to watch and take notes from educators such as Dr. Maxwell Maltz, Harold Camping, Les Brown, Anthony Robbins, Napoleon Hill, Dale Carnegie, and many others via videos, including those through TED talks, live mentors, and digital mentors.

I began to create my journey videos, which I call "Personal video therapy." I shared my story of change and progress through my videos; this process sped up curiosity and confidence, and I saw it influencing others too.

I would also watch and critique myself through my videos. I noticed others commenting, letting me know that my videos were helping them.

A few individuals here and there would subscribe to my YouTube channel and comment that I was helping them, and that was encouraging for me. I was on to something!

I kept doing it, and here I am today, free!

Now, this is a suggestion because I know not everyone will be willing to do everything I've done. Our path is not even the same in life but I hope that even just one or two of these life-hacks I'm sharing with you are helpful, educational, and life-changing.

Here is a positive suggestion for you. Download online videos of any of the above educators. You can also go on, if you wish, to create your own YouTube channel for personal development, keeping it private or sharing it if you so desire. It will help you build confidence too, believe me.

My YouTube channel has many playlists that have most of these videos that have helped me over the years you're welcome to check them out @ Soldiersofselfmastery on Youtube.

SUBSTITUTING OTHER HELPFUL ACTIVITIES IN PLACE OF GAMBLING

I have just a short, helpful exercise for you.

Make a list of at least five reasons (could be more than that but not less) you gamble and from your list of interests you outlined in chapter one, find an alternative activity you can engage in when the urge to gamble comes.

For example;

The reason why I gamble	Alternative helpful activity
1. Feelings of boredom and loneliness 2. To provide excitement 3. Escape from problems or issues 4. Frustration 5. To stay focused	1. I watch a movie, write, or read a book 2. Hangout with a friend or invite friends over 3. Meditation 4. Talk to someone close to me 5. Set long and short term goals

Make it fun! Try yours now, and see many benefitting activities in which you can engage in place of gambling. Once you've done that take some time to try one of these activities you have listed. Have fun!

CHAPTER FOUR: Become Better And Stronger Using Self-talk

---

it's all about the story we tell ourselves.

It's so good to have you back! In this chapter, I will be sharing with you another tool for you to experience transformation, and that is practicing positive, self-talk. Sit tight!

Let me share a proverb with you, Proverbs 18:21

"Death and life are in the power of the tongue, and they that love it shall eat the fruit thereof."

Most of my life, I've been speaking harmful and deadly things to myself and others around me. When I realized how much I could accomplish simply by working on my talk, those negative words became more positive ones. It was terrific and inspiring. 'You eat what you speak'.

I jumped on this and paid closer attention to my words and what I was saying. I wanted positive results quicker. I got creative and took my self-talk to an entirely new level, which took me to a higher level of thinking.

Positive self-talk or positive inner dialogue is one of the easiest life-hacks you can use today. I call it PST for short.

PST used effectively will make you unstoppable!

Will implementing PST be easy? That's up to you to decide. But remember that what you say from this point onward is going to make a big difference in the outcome of your circumstances and your attitude toward life.

Let me ask you this, what are the things you are saying to yourself? Who are you? What names are you calling yourself? A soldier, a drunk, a loser, smart, creative, a great leader, lazy, a super dad, a super mom, or a problem gambler, an addict?

WHAT IS YOUR LABEL?

You and I are a product of labels both positive and negative. When we communicate them to ourselves, that's what we eventually become.

Most people have the wrong vision because of a faulty label someone put on them or some title they have adopted out of ignorance, through an experience we created or something life just threw at us earlier on in life.

What did your parents call you? One label can change how you see yourself. I recall an event that took place one summer afternoon.

My early childhood buddy, who is now deceased, I will call him T, and I were walking down our main 2-way street in between apartments one afternoon and we passed by a vehicle that had several older men inside. One man in the car had big ears and my friend said something to him as they were driving by. We knew these guys in the car.

T jokingly called one man in the car "hey ears," (Orejas in Spanish), it humiliated him. A long story short, later on, that afternoon, "ears" was working on a car beside other guys in a parking lot and they had fresh oil in a little bottle that usually had rum in it.

T and I were walking by, and he was threatened by this guy with the big ears, as he said, "don't you ever call me ears again!" To say the least, this guy was humiliated, and he probably went on carrying that self-image (although I'm not sure of this), but he almost beat up my friend. In fact, I remember them giving my friend a drink from the bottle that they had poured fresh oil into.

My buddy asked for a swig thinking it was rum, he took a good swig and didn't realize he was drinking oil until he tasted it and he spit it out, and all these guys started laughing at T.

Labeling someone or calling them names is not a good thing.

Labels become a significant part of our inner dialogue, becoming a personal vision of who we believe we are.

With your vocabulary, you hypnotize yourself into a state; this can be either positive or negative depending on the words or the label. If you continue with your negative self-talk, you will not grow, your speech has a lot to do with your growth in life.

Most people's communication is so derogatory most of the time that it destroys their happiness. Negative self-talks destroy what little confidence you have. It comes out in your conversations with others, and it holds you back, stopping you from reaching your full potential or coming to your self-realization.

In my personal life, I work on perfecting the art of listening because I have a higher level of awareness today. I have become more sensitive within myself, and when I am around others. Friend, you need to do that too.

My ears perk up like a wild animal in survival mode. I correct myself as quickly as possible when I notice deadly words coming out of my mouth, especially in the presence of other people. I simply bring the words to awareness and remind myself silently as much as possible.

This is exactly what we're talking about here. Take full possession of your tongue!

For example, if you continue to call yourself a failure, what impact do you think that will make? You will probably wind up as a failure. How does that make you feel?

Is it possible you have believed in some negative labels and have made them into a mental image of yourself?

It's time you erase such a mindset and start building new positive ones.

A Scribe once wrote: "Say those things that are not as if they are."

Speak life to yourself even if you're alone, express yourself, and let your mind and others know you mean business.

TRIGGERS AND TEMPTATIONS.

Temptation can't beat a mind that's made up!

A single-minded person is very stable during the time of testing!

Would you depend on instability? Of course not! It's like trying to walk with two broken feet.

What you can do instead is to prepare yourself for these events ahead of time because they will come! These are your challenges! Don't let them in, be obsessed to defeat this enemy, tap into that inner anger to win over this thing!

Triggers and temptations are the tests that show up at your door once you have finally decided that you will move in a productive direction, expect to be tested!

Passing the test will make you a better and stronger person. One must be prepared, as I said the tests will come, and you will have to face them head-on. This is how you're going to build more self-belief, enormous courage, and momentum.

Whatever you learn on the mountaintop, make sure you take it into the valley with you. And conversely, what you learn in the valley, make sure you take that with you up to the mountaintop.

Triggers are those things that are going to pop up and question your validity, direction, or purpose and most people are not prepared, so they are caught by surprise! Well, it no longer has to be a surprise!

The more you prepare for them, obviously, the more ready you will be to break through them and the less influence they will have!

By mentally and verbally reminding yourself that there will be little bumps along your journey, you'll be able to jump over them quickly. These bumps will undoubtedly show up, but we don't plan to fail; we fail because we don't plan.

The wise can see what's ahead and make the necessary, quick adjustments to grow through the experience before reaching what is ahead.

Be prepared for life! This will make everything about you more exciting and help you gain your freedom day by day.

"Weapons for Gaining Control and Winning Over Challenges"

1985, Great Lakes, US Navy - I endured 12 weeks of mind-altering during boot camp. I became a US Navy soldier within 90 days. Now, there's a lot more that I can share with you here about those experiences, but I'll keep that for another time. I'm just going to share a few key things I learned about personal survival, and one great understanding is knowing what you're up against! Know your enemy. That is vital for your daily progress.

Someone once said, "You cannot escape from prison unless you know you're in one."

I learned how fast you could retrain your mind to produce a different lifestyle in just a short amount of time through self-discipline. Today, more than ever, I have genuinely come to appreciate the experiences that I've gone through in the past, especially this one that I just shared with you - that your mind can be trained to change in a short amount of time if done effectively and repetitively.

Understanding and implementing what you can use to better yourself has to be in play continually. In life, in any given situation, you must know what you're up against.

A question for you friend, are you a soldier? A soldier of thought, of speech, of emotional control, a Soldier of Self Mastery?

Soldiers work on having a readiness mindset. Soldiers think quickly and effectively. They utilize weapons to defeat the enemy. Likewise, you need to have Life-hacks/Weapons/Tools/Exercises if you want to overcome this horrible addiction.

Here are a few tools and life-hacks to help you gain control and overcome addiction.

1. Stay away from comparing yourself to others.
A famous basketball player was asked during an interview, what makes you so great? Why are you so competitive? He answered I recognize that my competition is not others, it's myself. I compete with myself to become better than who I was yesterday.

Steve Jobs quote: "I have looked in the mirror every morning and asked myself, "if today were the last day of my life, would I want to do what I am about to do today?" And when the answer has been "No" for too many days in a row, I know I need to change something."

Compare yourself to who you were yesterday, and how you want to see yourself in the future.

2. Practice Mirror talk.
Get in front of a mirror whenever you have some available time and have a great conversation with yourself. Stare deep into your eyes, amazing things can happen at this moment, and you'll find this very rewarding as you continue to use this life-hack every day.

3. Think before giving advice.
Unless someone, one way or another, absolutely demands it from you. Providing advice to somebody when they're not ready to apply it may come back to bite you in the rear end! Instead, ask intelligent, open-ended questions. Doing this will entice your friend or family member to take more responsibility, and they will grow from this experience. This life-hack is not only for life coaches.

4. Be more consciously aware.

Practice being more sensitive to your inner being and your surroundings! This may save your life someday.

5. Believe you can become good at whatever it is that you want to achieve, believe!
This life-hack I'm sharing with you will help you achieve higher self-esteem.

6. Look deep within.
When you wake up while still on your bed or just before retiring (to sleep) while lying on your bed - look deep within. Are you presently heading to where you want to be in life?

Personally, I have found these are two of the best times to begin training your subconscious. You can go over your affirmations, you can watch a video, or you can do some reading. Remember, repetition is critical. Your mind is more pliable during these two periods.

7. Take time to be quiet with yourself.
Utilize 15-20 minutes a couple of times a week to simply think, and to listen to your heart, your inner voice. Cultivate this habit! Fine-tune your inner voice, keep notes about your thoughts. This is very rewarding at a very personal level. You have to experience it for yourself to know what it can do for you.

8. Practice the art of dominating your mind as much as possible.

Immediately dismiss thoughts that you don't want. I've heard it said that you have 5 seconds to make a decision (call it throwing a monkey wrench into the idea that is not serving you at the moment). Practice the art of mindfulness of your speech. Doing this day after day will help you dominate your mind. This ultimately results in taking control of your life. You will experience greater inner-joy.

9. Regular exercise will release much-needed endorphins within you!

(Great stuff) Include deep breathing several times a day! I'm not an expert in deep breathing, but I do know that when I practice it, something cool happens to me and it's super easy to do.

Deep breathing experts tell us about their research and the implementation of many great, quick therapeutic benefits that result from practicing deep breathing.

When I do this exercise, I experience more oxygen to my brain; therefore, it makes me feel excellent. Because your mind is energized and feels good, you feel good!

Practicing deep breathing anytime during the day will do this for you. This is something I highly recommend that you look into, do some additional research on this life-hack, it's worth it.

A short explanation of how I practice deep breathing.

Breathe in deep, holding the air inside a few seconds, or longer, you decide, and then you exhale!! As you inhale slowly, you can concentrate, think of positive thoughts, think of good things coming into you with each inhale and when you exhale, let go of the negative, bad experiences, bitterness, unforgiveness, etc.

Deep breathing can accomplish many wonderful miracles and healing inside of you, resulting in many health benefits for you. I encourage you to research the benefits of deep breathing; you will find some exciting things. Real wealth is good health.

A NEW YOU!!!

Visualize it, see it, begin to experience it! A new you is arising, one that speaks positivity. Your mind has a great ability for tapping into this new version of you, so breathe, reach within yourself, you are capable of more than you can imagine.

Most of the ideas and philosophies within this book are not new; some of them are things you might have seen before but didn't make use of them. Now you have a fresh start, a unique opportunity to grab hold of them, I urge you not to discount them.

Put your heart into it and see what treasures you can withdraw from yourself.

Swami Sivananda wrote: "Put your heart, mind, and soul into even your smallest acts. This is the secret of success."

Take a break and affirm this right now:

I am courageous!
I am confident!
I can create a life I love
I make positive choices for myself
I am in charge of how I feel
My possibilities are endless
I am making myself proud
I am regaining all I have lost
I am free from gambling addiction
I am free from self-doubt and filled with self-confidence
Though the storms rage and the wind blows, I will persevere
I am setting a positive mindset, and it will go brilliantly.

Language, words, the right ones elevate you!
That was awesome, was it not?

One of the most wonderful missions life can offer you is your personal transformation. What do you think will happen to you now that you have changed your focus from negative self-talk to a positive one?

I will leave you to experience and share your testimony, until then, don't stop affirming good things, your transformation is here, it is now!!

CHAPTER FIVE: A Better Habit Equals A Better You

One way to discover your potential and achieve exploits in life is through the development of healthy, helpful habits.

Developing good habits takes discipline, courage, and hard work. It also requires consistency daily to keep those habits in place. It makes perfect sense to cultivate habits that will help create a path to success, yet, we find that some patterns are very difficult to adopt.

That is mostly dependent on the individual's will, self-discipline, and determination, but all these have been found to fail so many times.

I heard the story of a guy who was quite overweight and wanted to lose some weight. Knowing how much he liked eating doughnuts, he changed the usual route he took to drive to work to avoid driving by Krispy Kreme doughnuts. He did this successfully for three weeks, and all his coworkers were proud of him. Then one day, he came to work with five boxes of hot Krispy Kreme doughnuts, three doughnuts already consumed.

Everyone started getting on his case for falling off the wagon. He smiled and said, "Wait, these are special doughnuts! I accidentally drove by Krispy Kreme this morning, and I could see the sign was lit up, telling me doughnuts were being made fresh. So I prayed, Lord, if you want me to have some of these incredible doughnuts, let me have a parking space right in front of the store! And sure enough, after driving around the block eight times, there it was!"

In the everyday battle of building a healthy habit, where we have everywhere filled with temptations and situations waiting for you to compromise your determination, you might want to make the part of the Lord's prayer which says... "lead me not into temptation"... a daily recitation.

My opinion… I know!

Your daily growth depends on the type of habits you keep, which in turn determines the pattern your life follows. Your habits include how you spend your time, the things you give high priority in your life, and the goals you set for yourself.

More often it is advised that you set short term goals, especially goals that can be attained in a day because this brings about your daily growth, a way of measuring your performance, and that eventually, builds a healthy, successful lifestyle for you.

Although the strategy of setting short term goals is suitable for measuring performance, we wouldn't be adopting that strategy in breaking addictions. Instead, we would be looking at how to focus on repeatedly performing the desired behavior.

Habits require time to be perfectly developed, and it is particularly hard in the early stages of development. So rather than trying so hard to achieve a certain level of performance, which could be deteriorating and eventually, hinder the process of building your habits because of weak willpower and self-control, you should instead focus on practicing your desired habit daily.

We will be looking at three stages of building your desired habits, and the first stage applies to any habit at all, not just gambling, so you can use these same strategies to tackle any other problem habits that you have.

STAGE 1: RECOGNIZING YOUR PROBLEM HABITS

In chapter two of this book, we talked about self-realization, where you have to realize that you have a destructive addiction and are ready to make a change.

To build your desired habits, you must first identify your problem habits and that, of course, is the core topic of this book - gambling and addiction.

Furthermore, the questions below will help you understand your problem habits so you can find a practical solution.

i) Why do you continue these habits?
Unless you understand the root cause of a problem, you will only be dealing with it superficially. Knowing the reason or cause of a problem makes it easier for you to tackle it.

For example, I smoke to deal with self-esteem issues. The root cause of smoking addiction here is self-esteem issues. I want to feel that I belong, I want to be able to look anyone in the eye. This will be a direct result of the environment I find myself in and the kind of people I mingle with.

That is a root cause. Now, I know the reason for the root cause and where to start my solution plan.

ii) What harm has these habits caused you?
Emotion is a very powerful tool that can help in putting away one habit and building another. The twin power emotions of pain and pleasure are powerful tools to help you lose interest in your old patterns so that you can create new helpful ones.

How does this work?

Whenever you think of your old habits, for instance, a gambling addiction, think of all the pain gambling caused you. Your brain is naturally wired to avoid whatever brings pain.

Then you can go ahead and think of the pleasure you would derive from quitting gambling and adopting new habits, what your life will be like without the gambling addiction.

You can try this tip during your meditation hours, where you envision yourself achieving as much as you want in life. Doing this always automatically rewires your brain to avoid that old habit and stick to the new, helpful ones that will help you achieve your dreams.

STAGE 2: CHOOSE YOUR DESIRED HABIT(S) TO REPLACE YOUR PROBLEM HABIT(S)

How else can the need or desire for your old habits be met?

We carried out an exercise where we mentioned the reasons for gambling and in contrast to it, what other helpful activities can take the place of gambling and in turn, satisfying your need at that time.

That is the answer you will be providing for this question, and if you carried out the exercise at first, you can just refer to it.

You have identified your problem habits, including why you engage in those habits and how bad you've had to suffer at the hands of these habits. Now you badly want to replace them with other helpful habits, but the mistake most people make here and which eventually frustrates their efforts on building new habits is that the new habits they choose are, although helpful, but not effective.

How can a habit be helpful but not effective?

Remember our aim here is to ultimately make you get rid of any desire to gamble again, so your new habit should provide you as much satisfaction if not more than what you derive from your problem habits.

What happens when you do not get the satisfaction you need from your new habits? You eventually become frustrated, give up hope, and fall back to the same old patterns.

So, in choosing new habits, make sure it is one that's not just helpful but effective enough to make you lose interest or desire in your old habits. Also, you will find these tips helpful.

i) Deal with one problem habit at a time if you have more than one problem habit. Usually, that should be the one with the most significant impact.

For instance, you have a gambling addiction and you also like to procrastinate on your to-do tasks. Here you have two problem habits to tackle. The best thing is to deal with the one that has a more pressing impact. To do this, you have to carefully weigh your losses to each of these problem habits. Which has caused you more pain? That's the one you want to work on first.

All this is in an attempt not to get yourself overwhelmed, distracted, or eventually frustrated, but some of these habits are chain-like, where one affects the other. Like a procrastination habit problem, if you do not tackle that, you might even end up procrastinating on cultivating new habits. Although that is unless they haven't caused you pain enough to make you determined.

However it works for you, just make sure you don't reach the point of falling back!

ii) What do you want to achieve? While identifying this, be as precise and detailed as you can be. You want to stop gambling! Well, why? That reason is certainly not enough to get you going. But check this out.

I want to quit gambling to build a meaningful life, which includes becoming a proud owner of my own business, building my own house, buying a car, and nurturing a strong relationship between my wife and kids. Because gambling has gotten in my way of doing all these, I want to quit! Get creative here! If I can you can.

Boom!!! Detailed and precise.

iii) Choose an adequate replacement habit that gets in your way of performing the old habits.

I can't overemphasize the importance of this, make sure your replacement habits are helpful and effective, and practical, and that they require providing as much satisfaction, even more, as you derived from the old habits.

STAGE 3: START YOUR ROUTINE

i) Try helpful little habits daily.
From your list of reasons why you engage in your old habits and the alternative activities you enjoy, choose one daily and try it. By doing so, you are building interest in your new habits and losing desires for your old ones.

For example, I gamble to escape problems and issues. Rather than gambling, I use meditation to escape from my problems and issues daily.

ii) Don't set yourself up for temptations, be accountable to someone.
Like the guy in our story who wanted to lose some weight, he set himself up for temptation by driving by Krispy Kreme. Many of us fall for temptations when building new habits, and we find ourselves back to where we started.

Your willpower, self-discipline, and determination will do well to save you here.

iii) Celebrate your progress.
Did you complete a day, week, or month without engaging in that old habit?
Good!!! Then reward yourself.

Maybe it didn't go smoothly, you fell and braced yourself, not once, not twice, you don't have to feel inadequate, celebrate the little progress you have made. Building new habits long term isn't achieved in a day, week, or month, it's a work in progress.

So, celebrate your progress, celebrate your wins, and give yourself a reward that will boost your energy to do more.

CHAPTER SIX: Building Wealth And Regaining All That's Lost

"The person who doesn't know where his next dollar is coming from usually doesn't know where his last dollar went."

As I mentioned earlier, if you find yourself stuck with gambling or any other form of addiction, chances are you're short of money, or perhaps you're in debt either through gambling or buying drugs or paying your bills. It bothers you and gives you a sleepless night.

Sound familiar?

You're not alone, getting stuck with gambling cost me a lot, it cost me money, got me in debt, and most importantly it cost me some important relationships and life opportunities.

The good news is, after recovering from my addiction, I was able to set the pace and get my life in order again. I paid off my debts, and I started working toward generating passive income and cash flow through the use of my God-given purpose.

And I want to help you do the same. Throughout the first 5 chapters of this book, I have given you the weapons and tools you need to end gambling and other addictions. Now let's talk about how to build wealth, pay your debts, and regain all that's lost.

Most affluent and successful people have three financial intentions:

To produce an excellent working income.

To generate massive passive income and cash flow.

To create financial freedom: no more worries about money.

Poor people, on the other hand, want a decent living. This is one of the key elements to building wealth that nobody tells you.

Let's get real here, can we? Having an average mindset about money in this day and age won't get you anywhere. You have to carry a winning mentality with you all the time. And winning as we might know it is not easy. Anybody that tells you winning is easy is probably lying to you or they have already gone through the hard work once and now winning is easy.

If you want to build wealth and achieve financial freedom, here are the key things you need to start putting into action in your life right now.

1) TAKE RESPONSIBILITY FOR YOUR FINANCIAL LIFE

"The price of greatness is responsibility." ~ Winston Churchill.

Say this out loud: "I am responsible for my financial life." This is the first step toward building financial freedom. You're responsible for your financial life, not your parents, spouse, children, or close friends.

There are two roles you must never abdicate the authority to anyone in life.

The driver's seat
The check

Taking financial responsibility means you're in charge of the financial decisions you make. If you gain money or lose it, you did that to yourself, not the economy or government. Thinking this way gives you an edge to get real and obsessed with yourself.

You must accept responsibility for your actions, results, and your mistakes. That is the first step toward building freedom.

2) DOUBLE YOUR MONEY

Ever heard the parable of the Three Servants? If you haven't here is it for you to digest:

There was a story of a man going on a long trip. He called together his servants and entrusted his money to them while he was gone. He gave five bags of silver to one, two bags of silver to another, and one bag of silver to the last—dividing it in proportion to their abilities. He then left on his trip.

The servant who received the five bags of silver began to invest the money and earned five more. The servant with two bags of silver also went to work and earned two more. But the servant who received the one bag of silver dug a hole in the ground and hid the master's money.

After a long time, their master returned from his trip and called them to give an account of how they had used his money. The servant to whom he had entrusted the five bags of silver came forward with five more and said, 'Master, you gave me five bags of silver to invest, and I have earned five more.

The master was full of praise. 'Well done, my good and faithful servant. You have been faithful in handling this small amount, so now I will give you many more responsibilities. Let's celebrate together!'

The servant who had received the two bags of silver came forward and said, 'Master, you gave me two bags of silver to invest, and I have earned two more.'

The Master said, 'Well done, my good and faithful servant. You have been faithful in handling this small amount, so now I will give you many more responsibilities. Let's celebrate together!'

Then the servant with the one bag of silver came and said, 'Master, I knew you were a harsh man, harvesting crops you didn't plant and gathering crops you didn't cultivate. I was afraid I would lose your money, so I hid it in the earth. Look, here is your money back.'

But the master replied, 'You wicked and lazy servant! If you knew I harvested crops I didn't plant and gathered crops I didn't cultivate, why didn't you deposit my money in the bank? At least I could have earned some interest on it.'

Then he ordered, 'Take the money from this servant, and give it to the one with the ten bags of silver. To those who use well what they are given, even more, will be given, and they will have an abundance. But from those who do nothing, even what little they have will be taken away.'

I encourage you to digest this story and let it sink in.

One of the fundamental principles of building long-lasting wealth is to know how to double your money. Let's analyze each servant's performance in the story you just read.

The first servant was given 5 bags of silver by the master and doubled it to 10 by proper investing. The law of doubling working here.

The second servant did the same and doubled his two bags of silver to four.

The third servant was given one bag of silver and refused to trade with it because he was afraid of losing the master's money, so he hid it in the ground.

Until you know how to double one dollar into two dollars, you can't accomplish much!

Is there any principle to attain wealth? A big yes to that and one of the most important things you must learn is the law of doubling.

The average millionaire in the world today attains financial freedom by applying the principle of the first and second servants while ordinary people focus on how to keep the money they have without the thought of investing it.

I learned an Important phrase from Grant Cardone, want to know what the phrase is? Here we go: "Money Gets Bored."

It literally means if you keep saving the little you have without multiplying it, get ready to lose it by one means or the other.

Most people think they can double their money by investing in luck! Doing things like rolling dice with their money, gambling it in the casino, or buying bitcoin currency. Don't invest money in luck. Instead, invest your money in physical assets. A visible asset could be buying land at a lower price and selling it at a higher price for profit.

A huge investment of my time and money went into this book you're holding, but the fact is, I know this book will make an impact on people's lives, make me some money, and will keep generating profit for my family even when I'm gone.

That, to me, is a visible asset, a proper way to invest because I can see the value even if I don't hold the cash yet. The thought that this book will do amazing things in your life alone gives more joy; it helps me feel that I am making progress utilizing my God-given purpose.

So, beginning now and going onward, start thinking about how you can double the money in your hand. Let's say you have $100 and you start thinking about how you can double it to $1000 through proper investing. If you don't know how to invest your money properly, then keep reading. I will teach you how before the end of our meetings in this book.

3) SET INTENTIONS

"Money is good for nothing unless you know the value of it by experience." P.T Barnum

The popular story that a journey of a thousand miles begins with a single step is so true and until you determine what goal you want to achieve and start doing everything you can towards achieving such goals, nothing works!

Setting financial intentions also means setting goals and then doing everything you can to achieve them. So let me ask you, have you determined your financial intentions yet? Do you have a five-year plan for your life and business? If your answer is no, then it's time to do some brainstorming. I challenge you to answer the questions below.

1: What will be your working income from your business 5 years from now?

2: What is your passive income from your business?

3: What are the five services you can render right now to get profit in return?

4: What value and legacy do you want to create 5 years from now?

5: What is the smallest step you can take to start getting things going?

Take your time to brainstorm and answer the questions above. Once you get that done, start taking important action toward achieving your goals.

Remember, if you shoot for the stars you'll at least hit the moon.

4) WHAT TO DO IF YOU DON'T HAVE ENOUGH MONEY TO START A BUSINESS

Don't have enough money to start your business? No problem. Rich people use creative financial methods to start a profitable business and I am going to teach you how to do the same thing.

Time for some brainstorming, answer the questions below:

If you don't have the capital to start your major business, what can you do right now to raise money?

For example, Grant Cardone once coached a 14-year-old boy how to turn $1000 into $10,000 by washing 90 affluent cars for 100 dollars each. If you don't want to wash a car, what are the things you can do? It could be buying a product and selling it for more than it cost. I want you to take your time here and brainstorm the things you can do to start generating income.

How can I get a sponsor or investor for my business?

If you have a good business plan, then you might want to get a sponsor or investor for your business... you can find a sponsor for your business and promise to promote their products in return or find an investor to fund the business. It's important to note that people usually won't do something unless they know how it will benefit them in one way or the other. So If you want people to quickly support you, show them how it will benefit them in return.

Use Fundraising: you can sign up to a website like Bonifer, or fundly, or edco. You can inform people what your business is about and have them support you. So many businesses have thrived today through the power of fundraising. If you can't do it on your own, let people do it for you.

Good debt vs Bad debt: most people borrow money and spend it on buying material things or for personal use. That is called bad debt. Good debt, on the other hand, is borrowing money and investing it for a profit. Borrowing money for personal use will put you in trouble and bring about more debt. Please, oh, please don't do that. Only borrow money when you have a good business strategy ready to deploy, and you need money for the marketing operation. For example, Apple borrows billions of dollars while sitting on 240 billion dollars in cash. That's the power of good debt. Borrow to expand and not to contrast.

Find a Business Partner: most successful businesses in the world today wouldn't have achieved their success without a partnership or shareholders. Mark Zuckerberg, CEO of Facebook, invited 5 people to his Harvard dorm room 9 years ago to discuss a business opportunity. Only 2 people showed up, and they got in. Today those two people are billionaires: Dustin Moskovitz $6.5 Billion and Eduardo Saverin $3.4 Billion. Mark could do the work, but he needed people that had money, so he had to look for business partners. You might want to do the same. If you can do the work, look for someone that has the money and venture with them. If you have the money, then you might want to look for people that can do the work.

5) STAY FOCUSED WHEN STRUGGLING

Most people tend to become indecisive when they're struggling or trying to achieve their financial goals. Rich people, on the other hand, know how to stay focused in the midst of the storm.

If you're losing money or your business is not generating income, stay focused, and work it out. Trying to do more won't provide the solution you crave. But if you learn how to utilize the little you have and do the work, you'll experience a significant transformation.

Don't let challenges scatter you, stay focused, and figure it out. If you can't manage stress and problems, you won't be able to achieve success.

CHAPTER 7: The Transformation Loop

If you made it to this stage, well done, give yourself some credit. You now have the tools and the ability to win over this horrible addiction and regain your life. In this chapter, I'm going to give you the transformation loop. Use it to keep the ball rolling and even make things better.

If you ever dream of living the good life, then this chapter is for you. Without wasting your time, let's get things started.

The Hard Realization

The first stage of transformation is coming to the hard realization of the situation you're presently in. As someone who wants to achieve, we all have to start somewhere on our journey to success. The start often feels incredible with so much power running through your body.

But then we hit an obstacle. Unexpected realities happen in our life. It could be an accident, a job that doesn't pay you well, a loss of a close relationship, or someone you love walks in and tells you they're no longer interested.

Whatever it is, hard realization happens in our lives. It's a time when you think, I've had enough and I am no longer doing this. When that happens, life shifts.

Most people at this stage quit and think things won't get better. They develop self-hatred, thinking they can't do anything right in life. We start thinking about all that could go wrong, the bills, the home, and the truth is at this stage real negativity sets in. Sound familiar? You're not alone.

When we hit the hard realization zone, which I think will happen to you if it hasn't happened already. When you find yourself building self-hatred, to survive, you need to do something important.

The Reverse Of Stacking

If you hit the zone I just mentioned, or a close friend or a family member did, the most important thing to do is to start the reverse of stacking. Simply take a pause, stop thinking about what could go wrong and start thinking about what could go right.

Ask yourself this question.

Who do I not want to be?

Write whatever comes to your mind. For me, I don't want to be someone who gives up before they win. I don't want to live a life of regrets. I don't want to be someone that my kids won't be proud of in the future, and most importantly, I don't want to be someone who walks through this earth without leaving a legacy. I don't want to be forgotten easily. But, well, that's just for me, what about you?

Who do I want to be? Who do you want to be?
I want to be someone who goes through the struggle. I want to be someone whose stories motivate millions of people not to give up. I want to be someone who helps others, someone who loves, and someone who forgives and moves on. But then again that's just for me, who do you want to be? Write it down.

If you answer these two questions thoroughly, you start gaining momentum and start becoming empowered, and now you start thinking about:

Your Compelling Future

Again I want you to answer a few questions here.

How can you serve? What problem can you solve?
The average successful person today provides quality service and solves a problem. I am solving a problem by investing time to write this book you're reading. What about you? Think critically about this and write your thoughts down.

Now, what would go wrong if you couldn't do these things? We tend to do a lot more when we think about pain. Feel the pain but then use it as motivation to take action.

Consciousness Engineering

"The key to growth is the introduction of higher dimensions of consciousness into our awareness." - Lao Tzu

This section completes the transformation loop by learning consciousness engineering. The mind is the most awesome tool a human possesses. The way you use your mind towards success determines how far you will go in life. The problem? Your mind has been programmed with so many beliefs that brought you to where you are in life today.

No matter how successful or tragic your life may be today, it's the manifestation of what you believe and how you've grown up to see the world. Because you see, our reality is being programmed by the world we live in. While other animals can start walking and thriving after birth, we humans have to live our life from birth depending on one thing or another.

As time goes on, this state of living creates our model of life and how the world perceives us. Frankly speaking, what you believe is true about life are the things that can move you or trigger your emotions.

So let me ask you these questions.

What is your perspective on life?

Does positivity or negativity trigger your emotions?

Have you retired from giving your best to the world?

You might want to consider taking some time to reflect on your life and figure out how you got to where you are now.

"Change your thoughts, and you change your world." - Norman Vincent Peale.

If you want to experience transformation, happiness, and long-lasting success in life, you need to grow to a higher level of consciousness. You need to become the awakening itself.

And that's precisely what consciousness engineering does for you. If you carefully study the new system for living that I'm about to show you in just a bit, you'll tap into an infinite power to solve all your life puzzles. You'll find ultra clarity and a higher purpose of living.

There are 12 critical pieces you need to engineer into your own life if you want to become a high performer and rapidly achieve your true potential. I want you to carefully rate how you're doing on each one using a scale of 1 - 10

1 represents weak, while 10 represents extraordinary. Don't stay on each piece for too long. The first answer that comes to your mind will usually be the best. So get your journal ready and let's dive deep into the 12 areas of your life to engineer your new system for living.

#1. Relationship: How happy are you in the relationship you're in right now? Can you name three things you've been grateful for in your relationship? Are you getting enough support from your partner to achieve your dream? I believe you know the best answer to this, so grab your notepad and record your answer.

#2. Achievers: Do you have at least 3 friends or connections that can help you get to the next level when it comes to reaching your potential?

#3. Adventure: How often do you explore the world? Are you the type driven by new things coming around you every day or do you long to explore new ideas that could create a fantastic moment in your life?

#4. State Of Mind: How often does your state of mind affect you and is it something that determines the outcome of your day?

#5. Your Health: Are you living a healthy life right now and do you exercise at least twice a week?

#6. Growth: How fast are you growing toward achieving your potential?

#7. Your Skills: How fast are you growing your skills and do you have the required skills to get to the next stage toward achieving the goals you have in place right now?

#8. Your Spiritual Life: How spiritually connected are you? Do you meditate, pray, or perform the right spiritual rituals that can connect you to a deeper level of nature?

#9. Career: Is your career advancing in the direction you want it to go? Are you climbing the ladder to the top right now in your life?

#10. Creativity: How creative are you in figuring things out? Are you problem-driven or solution-driven?

#11. Discipline: Are you disciplined and committed to the things you need to do to achieve your goals? Do you set a deadline to achieve something and do you meet it?

#12. Family: Do you arrange time out to be more valuable and committed to making your family happy? Again, you should answer this based on whatever family means to you right now.

Made it to this stage? Well done. You now have the twelve critical pieces that determine your level of performance in life. Now think about your answers to each one of the pieces above. What can you do to improve?

Start by noting five areas where you think you need to improve and urgently start working toward balancing those areas.

For example, if you scored a 3 for yourself in the area of discipline that means your level of discipline is critically low, and you should start thinking about how to move the score up.

Also, do the same for every piece mentioned above, first find out the areas where you're not doing well and start reflecting on how you can turn the situation around and work toward generating an excellent result.

Remember the right answer always comes from asking the right question. And there you have it, the 12 critical pieces of high-performance people.

That's it for the transformation loop. It's time to get to work! If you carefully do everything we talked about in this book, addictions and challenges won't terrify you ever again. The ball is in your court, you have been handed a new opportunity to turn your life around. My question is, how are you going to use it? This is not a motivational book, it's an action-driven book. I want you to start taking action right now and see the reward that awaits you.

Made in USA - Kendallville, IN
1162246_9781089617082
09.10.2020 0832